CHEMICALS IN ACTION

ACIDS AND BASES

Chris Oxlade

REVISED AND UPDATED

Heinemann Library

Chicago, Illinois

© 2002, 2007 Heinemann Library
a division of Reed Elsevier Inc.
Chicago, Illinois

Customer Service 888-454-2279
Visit our website at www.heinemannraintree.com

Editorial: Clare Lewis
Design: Steve Mead and Fiona MacColl
Picture Research: Hannah Taylor
Production: Julie Carter
Originated by Modern Age
Printed and bound in China by Leo Paper Group

11 10 09 08 07
10 9 8 7 6 5 4 3 2 1

New edition ISBN: 978-1-4329-0050-2 (hardcover)
                 978-1-4329-0057-1 (paperback)

The Library of Congress has cataloged the first edition as follows:
Oxlade, Chris
   Acids and bases / Chris Oxlade.
      p. cm. -- (Chemicals in action)
   Includes bibliographical references and index.
   ISBN 1-58810-194-0
   1. Acid-base chemistry--Juvenile literature. [1. Chemistry. 2.
   Acids. 3. Bases.] I. Title.
QD477 .O95 2001
546".24—dc21
                                        2001000102

Acknowledgments
The author and publishers are grateful to the following for permission to reproduce copyright material: Ace Photo Library p. **31**, Alamy Images pp. **6**, **39**, Andrew Lambert pp. **14**, **16**, **33**, Corbis pp. **13**, **22**, Edifice p. **18**, Environmental Images (Toby Adamson) p. **38**, Peter Gould pp. **11**, **24**, Photolibrary.com p. **35**, Robert Harding p. **30**, Roger Scruton pp. **10**, **32**, **36**, Science Photo Library pp. **4**, **9**, **12**, **18**, **19**, **28**, **34**, TDG Nexus (Mark Perry/ Simon Peachey) p.**5**, Trevor Clifford pp. **8**, **15**, **17**, **20**, **23**, **25**, **27**, **29**, **37**.

Cover photograph: a chemical strip in a glass measure reproduced with permission of Getty Images/The Image Bank.

The publishers would like to thank Ted Dolter and Dr. Nigel Saunders for their assistance in the preparation of this title.

Every effort has been made to contact copyright holders of any material reproduced in this book. Any omissions will be rectified in subsequent printings if notice is given to the publisher.

The paper used to print this book comes from sustainable sources.

Some words are shown in bold, **like this**. You can find out what they mean by looking in the glossary.

CONTENTS

CHEMICALS IN ACTION

What's the link between **corrosion**, cleaning the kitchen, bee stings, firefighting, and indigestion? The answer is acids and bases. All of these things contain acids or bases, or happen because of acids or bases. Our knowledge of how acids and bases behave is used in making chemicals, in farming, in engineering, and in our homes.

The study of acids and bases is part of the science of chemistry. Many people think of chemistry as something that scientists study by doing experiments in laboratories with special equipment. This aspect of chemistry is very important. It is how scientists determine what substances are made of and how they make new materials. However, this is only a small part of chemistry. Most chemistry happens away from laboratories, in factories and chemical plants. It is used to manufacture a wide range of items, such as synthetic fibers for fabrics, drugs to treat diseases, explosives for fireworks, solvents for paints, and **fertilizers** for growing crops.

Many acids and bases are found in nature. This green-looking lake in a volcano in Costa Rica is acidic.

About the experiments

There are several experiments for you to try. They will help you understand some of the chemistry in this book. An experiment is designed to help solve a scientific problem. Scientists use a logical approach to experiments so they can make conclusions from the results of the experiments. A scientist first writes down a hypothesis, which he or she thinks might be the answer to the problem, then designs an experiment to test the hypothesis. He or she writes down the results of the experiment and concludes whether or not the results show that the hypothesis is true. We only know what we do about chemistry because scientists have carefully carried out thousands of experiments over hundreds of years. Experiments have allowed scientists to discover that acids and alkalis exist, and how they react with each other and other chemicals.

DOING THE EXPERIMENTS

All the experiments in this book have been designed for you to do at home with everyday substances and equipment. They can also be done in your school science class. Always follow the safety advice given with each experiment. Ask an adult to help you when the instructions tell you to.

Acids or bases can be dangerous. Flasks, canisters, and tankers that contain them must display a hazard warning.

ABOUT ACIDS, BASES, AND ALKALIS

Acids and bases are chemicals, and you have probably seen bottles of both in the science classroom in your school. An alkali is simply a base that dissolves in water (you can find out more about the difference between bases and alkalis on page 11). You might also recognize some names of acids, bases, and alkalis, such as sulfuric acid and sodium hydroxide.

Acids, bases, and alkalis are not just chemicals found in bottles in laboratories. There are hundreds of natural acids, bases, and alkalis in plants and animals. For example, lemon juice contains an acid called citric acid, and you have hydrochloric acid in your stomach that is so strong it could eat away **metal**! Even wasp stings contain alkalis. Hundreds of

everyday substances, such as shampoo, vinegar, spray cleaners, and even rainwater, are acids, bases, or alkalis. They are also found in medicines, such as antacid tablets, and you can often see the names of acids, bases, and alkalis in the list of ingredients on packaging.

In factories, acids, bases, and alkalis are used to clean materials, such as metal. They are also the **raw materials** that make up hundreds of other chemicals, such as fertilizers and **detergents**.

◄ Oven cleaners contain strong acids or alkalis. It is important to wear protective gloves when using these cleaners.

Acid, base, and alkali reactions

Acids, bases, and alkalis can eat away other substances or make them fizz, because there is a reaction between them. For example, when acids come into contact with some metals, the metal is eaten away and bubbles of hydrogen are formed. Cleaning liquids that contain alkalis work because the alkali reacts with grease and turns it into other substances.

SAFETY WITH ACIDS, BASES, AND ALKALIS

Although some natural acids, bases, and alkalis are usually harmless to touch and eat, many acids, bases, and alkalis found in the laboratory and in household cleaners are dangerous. They are described as **corrosive** or **caustic**, which means they will eat away some materials, including your skin. Watch for hazard warning symbols on chemicals in the laboratory and at home. Never touch or taste any chemical unless you have been told by a scientist or other adult that it is safe to do so. Always wear safety glasses when using acids, bases, or alkalis.

Toxic

Corrosive

Irritant

Acids

The word acid comes from the Latin word *acidus*, which means "sour." Sour is the sharp taste in fruits such as lemons and oranges. One of the **properties** of an acid is that it tastes sour, which is how acids got their name. Lemons and oranges taste sour because they contain citric acid, which is a weak acid that is safe to taste. You should never taste an acid (or any other chemical) unless you are told that it is safe to do so by a scientist or other adult.

The other properties of acids are:
- acids are usually found dissolved in water
- acids can eat away other substances, such as metals, and they are described as corrosive
- acids are **neutralized** by alkalis and bases (this means that an alkali or a base turns an acid into a substance that is no longer an acid)
- acids have a **pH** below 7 and they also turn blue **litmus** paper red (you can find out about the pH scale and litmus paper on page 14).

Carbonated drinks are quite acidic. They can even be used to clean dirty coins!

Laboratory acids

The most common acids that scientists use in the laboratory are sulfuric acid, hydrochloric acid, and nitric acid. These are also the most common acids used in industry. The **chemical formulas** for these acids are:

sulfuric acid	H_2SO_4
hydrochloric acid	HCl
nitric acid	HNO_3

You can see from these formulas that all acids contain hydrogen. It is the hydrogen that gives them their properties. The formulas, though, do not tell you one very important thing, and that is that the chemicals must be dissolved in water before they have the properties of acids. For example, hydrochloric acid is made up of hydrogen chloride (HCl) dissolved in water. Pure hydrogen chloride is a gas. It is not an acid, but it Is called an **acidic gas** because it dissolves in water to make an acid.

Strong and weak acids

Some acids are weak and others are strong. Weak acids are relatively harmless because they are not very corrosive. The citric acid in fruit is an example of a weak acid. Strong acids, such as hydrochloric acid, are dangerous because they are corrosive.

Acids can be made weaker by mixing them with water. An acid with lots of water added is called a **dilute acid**, and an acid with only a little water is called a **concentrated acid**. Concentrated sulfuric acid is a strong acid; dilute sulfuric acid is a weak acid. However, citric acid is always a weak acid no matter how concentrated it is.

Concentrated sulfuric acid is nasty stuff! It dehydrates (removes the water from) sugar instantly.

9

Bases and alkalis

You can think of bases and alkalis as the chemical opposites of acids. A base is any substance that will neutralize an acid. This means that adding a base to an acid eventually turns the acid into a liquid that is not an acid.

An alkali is a base that will dissolve in water to make a **solution**. However, some bases do not dissolve in water. They are called **insoluble bases**. This means that all alkalis are also bases, but only bases that dissolve in water are alkalis. For example, magnesium oxide and calcium oxide are both bases because they both neutralize acids. But magnesium oxide does not dissolve in water, so it cannot be an alkali, too. Calcium oxide does dissolve in water, so it is an alkali.

Properties of alkalis

The most obvious property of an alkali is that it feels soapy or slimy to the touch. You should never touch (or taste) an alkali unless you are told that it is safe to do so by a scientist or other adult.

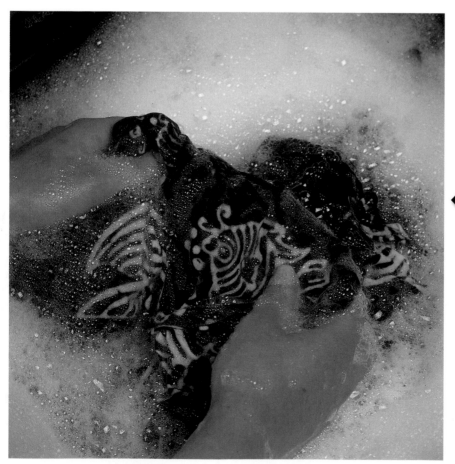

Some alkalis and bases are good cleaning agents. This liquid contains the base ammonia (NH_3).

The other properties of alkalis are:
- alkalis can eat away other substances, such as metals, and they are described as corrosive
- alkalis are neutralized by acids (this means that an acid turns an alkali into a substance that is no longer an alkali)
- alkalis have a pH above 7 and they also turn red litmus paper blue (you can find out about the pH scale and litmus paper on page 14).

The word alkali comes from the Arabic *al-qili*, which is the word for the ashes made when certain plants are burned. People first got alkalis from these ashes.

Laboratory bases and alkalis

The most common alkalis that scientists use in the laboratory are sodium hydroxide and calcium hydroxide. They are also the most common alkalis used in industry. Sodium hydroxide is also known as caustic soda, and calcium hydroxide is also known as slaked lime.

The chemical formulas for these alkalis are:

sodium hydroxide	$NaOH$
calcium hydroxide	$Ca(OH)_2$

You can see from these formulas that alkalis contain hydrogen and oxygen combined into an OH, and it is this OH that gives them their properties. The formulas do not tell you one very important thing, and that is that the chemicals must be dissolved in water before they show the properties of alkalis. For example, the alkali sodium hydroxide is made up of sodium hydroxide, which is a white solid, dissolved in water. Solid sodium hydroxide is not an alkali, but is called an **alkaline** solid because it dissolves in water to make an alkaline solution.

The base calcium oxide dissolves in water to make an alkaline solution that turns litmus paper blue.

Natural acids, bases, and alkalis

All plants and animals contain thousands of chemicals, including many acids, bases, and alkalis. These acids, bases, and alkalis play a part in important processes that allow plants and animals to live and grow, such as **digestion**. Some plants and animals also use acids, bases, and alkalis for self-defense.

Acids and alkalis in your body

Did you know that your stomach is like a bag full of acid? It contains up to 1 pint (0.5 liter) of hydrochloric acid that helps you digest food! The acid is part of a liquid called gastric juice that helps break down the complex chemicals found in food into simpler substances that your body can digest. Hydrochloric acid also kills any bacteria on the food and is strong enough to dissolve metals and burn skin. Fortunately your stomach has a special lining that protects it from the acid, and your body also makes alkalis that neutralize the acid so that it doesn't eat away your intestines!

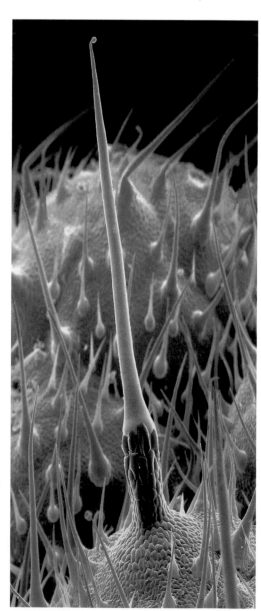

Your body also uses different acids to grow and work. Vitamin C is a chemical that helps to grow skin and healthy bones and heal wounds, but it is actually an acid called ascorbic acid. Fruit and vegetables are an important source of vitamin C.

The stings on nettle plants inject a tiny amount of acid into your skin!

Some acids in your body are made by other **organisms**, including the bacteria that live in your mouth and feed on tiny pieces of food. They produce acid that can eat away at your teeth and cause decay. Regular brushing keeps too many bacteria from growing.

Acid and alkali stings

Ants, bees, and nettle plants can all sting you by injecting tiny amounts of acid into your skin. Ants inject formic acid (also known as methanoic acid). Wasp stings, on the other hand, contain alkali instead of acid. Stings swell up because your body sends water to the area of the sting to try to dilute (weaken) the acid or alkali. Acids and alkalis are also used to treat bites and stings. You can find out how they do this on page 36.

Naturally occurring calcium carbonate is turned into lime using fire at this lime kiln.

MAKING LIME

Calcium **carbonate** ($CaCO_3$) is a chemical that makes up many types of rock, including chalk and limestone. It is a base and an important raw material for the chemical industry. Heating calcium carbonate makes it decompose into carbon dioxide and calcium oxide, commonly known as lime. Lime was one of the first human-made chemicals, and it has been used since Roman times to make cement for building. There is more about lime on page 36.

TESTING ACIDS AND ALKALIS

Scientists often need to find out whether a substance is an acid, an alkali, or neutral. A neutral substance is a substance that is neither an acid nor an alkali.

Scientists test substances using chemicals called **indicators**. When an indicator is put in a liquid, it changes color to show whether the liquid is an acid, an alkali, or neutral. Some indicators show only whether a liquid is an acid or an alkali, while others show how strong an acid or alkali is. Indicators can only be used with liquids, so you cannot test a solid substance with an indicator.

Acid or alkali?

Litmus is an indicator that shows whether a liquid is an acid or an alkali, and it comes in the form of paper strips, called litmus paper, or in a **solution**. Here's what happens when litmus paper is dipped in acids, alkalis, and neutral liquids:

	In acid	In alkali	In neutral
Red litmus	Stays red	Turns blue	Stays red
Blue litmus	Turns red	Stays blue	Stays blue

Red litmus paper turns blue when it is dipped into an alkaline solution.

EXPERIMENT: NATURAL INDICATORS

Problem

Can acids and alkalis be tested without litmus paper?

Hypothesis

The chemical dyes in litmus paper come from a plant, so there might be similar dyes in other plants as well. Extracting dyes from plants and adding them to acids and alkalis will show if they are indicators.

EQUIPMENT
- red cabbage
- glass bowl
- large jar
- strainer
- small jars
- white vinegar
- tap water

Experiment steps

1 Pull some large leaves from the outside of a red cabbage, tear into small strips and place in a bowl. Ask an adult to help you pour roughly 1 pint (0.5 liter) of boiling water over the leaves.

2 Leave the water and cabbage mixture to cool (for about half an hour) before pouring it through a strainer into a large jar. This liquid is your indicator.

3 Add a few drops of the indicator to a small jar of tap water and to another of white vinegar (which is a weak acid). Note the color changes for both.

Results

What colors does the cabbage juice turn in the tap water and the weak acid? Are the colors the same? What do you think this shows about the cabbage juice? You can check your results on page 47.

Strong or weak?

The strength of an acid or alkali is measured on a scale called the **pH** scale that goes from 0 to 14. A liquid with a pH of 7 is neutral. A liquid with a pH lower than 7 is an acid. The lower the number, the more acidic it is, so pH 6 is a very weak acid and pH 0 is a very strong acid. A liquid with a pH higher than 7 is an alkali. The higher the number the more strongly alkaline it is. So pH 8 is a very weak alkali and pH 14 is a very strong alkali.

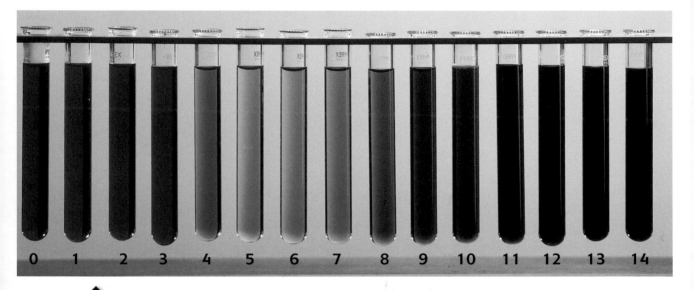

0   1   2   3   4   5   6   7   8   9   10   11   12   13   14

The test tubes contain acids (on the left) and alkalis (on the right) together with universal indicator solution. The strengths of the acids and alkalis are shown below as a pH number.

Universal indicator

An indicator called **universal indicator** shows the pH of a liquid. Like litmus, universal indicator comes in the form of paper strips, or as a **solution**. When it is put in a colorless liquid, it changes color to show how acidic or alkaline the liquid is. The pH is shown on a color-coded strip supplied with the indicator. Universal indicator is no good for testing colored liquids, because the indicator may get some of its color from the liquid.

EXPERIMENT: USING INDICATORS

Problem

How can a liquid be tested to see if it is acidic, alkaline, or neutral?

Hypothesis

Dipping litmus paper into a liquid will show whether a liquid is either acidic or alkaline. Dipping universal indicator into a liquid will show how weak or strong it is.

EQUIPMENT
- litmus paper (red and blue)
- universal indicator paper
- small jars
- substances to test, for example: apple juice, white vinegar, tap water, soap dissolved in a little water, lemon juice, rainwater, carbonated drinks, baking powder dissolved in water, toothpaste dissolved in some warm water

Experiment steps

1 Pour a small amount of the test substance into a small jar.

2 Dip a strip of red litmus paper into the liquid. If the dipped part turns blue the substance is alkaline. If it stays red it is either acidic or neutral. If it does stay red, dip a strip of blue litmus paper into the liquid. If the dipped part turns red the liquid is acidic, if it stays blue it is neutral. Repeat this process for each liquid and chart the results.

3 Next, dip a strip of universal indicator paper into each liquid, remove the paper, and place it next to the color strip supplied with the book of paper. If there is no exact color match, estimate the pH of the solution. Add the results to your table.

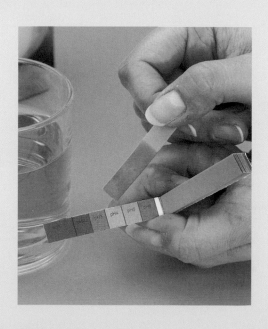

Results

Litmus paper and universal indicator paper show whether a liquid is acidic or alkaline, and how strongly acidic or alkaline it is.

ACID REACTIONS

When you put another substance into an acid, or pour an acid over another substance, a **chemical reaction** often occurs between the acid and the substance. During the reaction, new substances are formed. There is always a pattern of behavior to the reactions that happen between acids and other substances. For example, all acids react with the metal magnesium, and the products of the reaction are always hydrogen gas and a **compound** containing the magnesium. The reaction will be the same no matter what acid you use. Sometimes there is no reaction between an acid and a substance. For example, some types of plastic never react with any acid. This is also a pattern of behavior.

▲ Acids are used to dissolve scrap metal during the recycling process.

When you know the patterns of behavior that occur between acids and other substances, you can make a good guess about what is going to happen when you add an acid to a substance. When you add acid to a mystery substance, you can get some clues about what it could be by the reaction that occurs. For example, if you added acid to a piece of metal and there was no hydrogen produced, then you would know that the metal was not magnesium. So acids can be used as part of a series of laboratory tests on a substance.

Some useful reactions to know about are the reactions between acids and different metals, the reactions between acids and substances called **carbonates**, and the reactions between acids and bases or alkalis.

Reactions of acids and metals

When acids are added to some metals, the metals fizz and are eaten away. The fizzing is caused by tiny bubbles of hydrogen gas being formed—the hydrogen comes from the acid. The other part of the acid combines with the metal to make a compound called a **salt**. This is the general word equation for this reaction:

$$\text{acid} + \text{metal} \rightarrow \text{salt} + \text{hydrogen}$$

Here is an example:

hydrochloric acid	+ zinc	$\rightarrow$	zinc chloride	+ hydrogen
$2HCl$	+ Zn	$\rightarrow$	$ZnCl_2$	+ H_2

The reaction between a metal and an acid is an example of a **displacement reaction**. This is because the metal takes the place of, or displaces, the hydrogen in the acid. However, not all metals react with acids. You can find out why on page 22.

◀ Zinc and hydrocholoric acid react to produce bubbles of hydrogen.

EXPERIMENT: REACTIONS OF METALS AND ACIDS

Problem

What gas is produced when acids react with metals?

Hypothesis

Acids contain hydrogen, so the gas produced may be hydrogen. If a flame is put in the gas, it should burn with a pop if it is hydrogen.

EQUIPMENT
- plastic container
- plastic tube with lid (cake decorations come in suitable containers)
- white vinegar
- galvanized (zinc-coated) nails such as plasterboard nails or fencing nails
- safety match

Experiment steps

1 Lay the plastic tube on its side in the plastic container. Pour just enough vinegar into the container so that the plastic tube is completely filled with vinegar.

2 Put two or three nails into the plastic tube. Turn the plastic tube upside down so that the open end stays in the vinegar. If you do it carefully, the tube will stand on its end in the plastic container, full of vinegar, with the nails inside it.

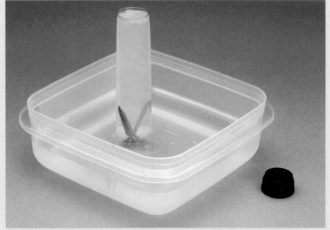

3 Bubbles of gas will soon start to come off the nails. Leave the experiment until you have about ½–1 inch (1–2 centimeters) of gas trapped in the top of your tube. This might take about 45 minutes.

4 Put the lid of the tube into the vinegar. Lift the plastic tube just enough to slide the lid into the open end—don't let any air get in! Once the lid is on, take the tube out of the vinegar. Dry the outside of the tube with a paper towel, and wash your hands.

5 Get an adult to help you with this step. You will only get one chance to get this part right! Turn the tube upright so that the lid is at the top. Light a safety match, take the lid off the tube and quickly hold the flame over the mouth of the tube. Listen carefully.

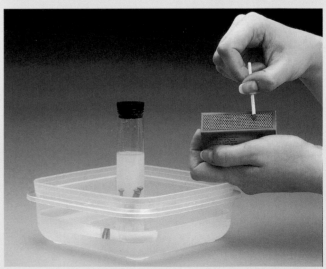

Results

When you hold the flame next to the tube, what sort of sound do you hear? What do you think this tells you about the gas in the tube? You can check your results on page 47.

| zinc | + | hydrochloric acid | $\rightarrow$ | zinc chloride | + | hydrogen |
| Zn | + | 2HCl | $\rightarrow$ | $ZnCl_2$ | + | H_2 |

The reactivity series

Different metals react with acids at different speeds. When acids are added to some metals, such as magnesium, there is a lot of fizzing, showing that the reaction between the acid and metal is very fast. Some metals, such as potassium, react so violently that they cause an explosion. This is because the reaction produces so much heat that the hydrogen gas given off by the reaction explodes. When acids are added to other metals, such as iron, there is only slight fizzing. This shows that the reaction between the acid and the metal is slow. This difference in the speeds of the reactions is an example of a trend in properties. Some metals, such as gold, do not react with acids at all.

The **reactivity series** is a list of common metals in order of how fast they react with acids. The most reactive metals, such as potassium and sodium, are at the top, and the least reactive, such as gold and silver, are at the bottom.

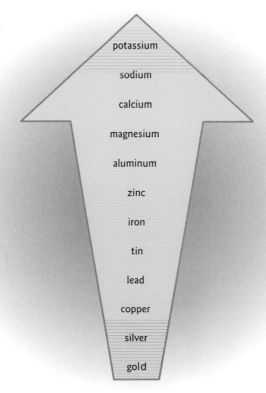

The reactivity series of common metals. It shows, for example, that aluminum is more reactive than zinc, but less reactive than magnesium.

21

Hydrogen in the reactivity series

The reactivity series shows how reactive a metal is. The metals at the top of the series are very reactive, and those at the bottom are not very reactive. Each metal in the series is more reactive than the one below it.

If you look at the list below, you will see that there is a point at which metals stop reacting with acids. This is because a metal will only react with an acid if it is more reactive than hydrogen. If it is more reactive, a displacement reaction takes place and the metal pushes the hydrogen out of the acid. If the metal is less reactive than hydrogen, then it cannot push the hydrogen out, and there is no reaction.

Hydrogen is often added to the reactivity series, even though it is not a metal. If an acid is added to a metal above hydrogen in the series, a reaction takes place and the metal displaces the hydrogen to make a salt. If an acid is added to a metal below hydrogen in the series, no reaction takes place.

Metal	Symbol	Reaction with acids
potassium	K	
sodium	Na	
calcium	Ca	
magnesium	Mg	All react
aluminum	Al	with acids
zinc	Zn	
iron	Fe	
lead	Pb	
hydrogen	H	
copper	Cu	No reaction
silver	Ag	with acids
gold	Au	

EXPERIMENT: REACTIVE METALS

Problem

Which common metals are most reactive?

Hypothesis

To find out which metals are most reactive, we can put pieces of the metals in a weak acid and watch what happens. The one that fizzes most quickly will be the most reactive.

EQUIPMENT

- nail or screw made of iron or steel
- galvanized (zinc-coated) nail or screw
- nail or screw made of copper or brass
- white vinegar (colored vinegar will work)
- three small jars
- one bowl (large enough to place the jars into)

Experiment steps

1 Put a nail or screw into each of the three small jars. Pour just enough vinegar into the jars to cover the nails or screws. Watch what happens over the next few minutes. While you are waiting, ask an adult to heat a pot of water (it does not need to boil).

2 Make sure a window is open because the next part gets really smelly! Ask the adult to pour some hot water into the bowl. Carefully put your jars into the water so that the hot water will heat up the vinegar in the jars. Again, watch what happens over the next few minutes. Do not breathe deeply near the warm vinegar.

3 Make a note of your results. If bubbles are coming off the surface of the metal, there is a reaction happening. You can make sure by gently swirling the vinegar to remove any bubbles. Then watch to see if they start coming off on their own again. Write down whether the reaction is fast, steady, or slow, or if there is no reaction at all.

4 Write down the three metals in order of their speeds of reaction, starting your list with the most reactive and working down to the least reactive. This is your reactivity series.

Results

Which metal fizzes most quickly? Which fizzes the least? What does this tell you about the reactivity of the different metals? Check your results on page 47.

Acids and carbonates

Just as there is a pattern of reactions between acids and metals, there is also a pattern of reactions between acids and carbonates. Carbonates are compounds made up of **atoms** of one **element**, combined with another group of atoms made up of one carbon atom and three oxygen atoms. One of the common carbonates is calcium carbonate. It makes up rocks such as chalk, marble, and limestone. Its formula is $CaCO_3$, and it is the CO_3 part that means it is a carbonate.

When an acid is added to a carbonate, the carbonate fizzes. This fizzing is caused by the bubbles of carbon dioxide gas formed in the reaction. Carbon dioxide is one of the products of the reaction. The other products are always water and a compound called a salt.

Here is the general equation for the reaction:

> **acid + carbonate   → salt + water + carbon dioxide**

For example, if hydrochloric acid is added to the rock marble, which is made up of calcium carbonate, the marble fizzes as carbon dioxide gas is made.

> **hydrochloric + calcium   →   calcium + water + carbon**
> **acid   carbonate   chloride   dioxide**
>
> $2HCl \quad + \quad CaCO_3 \quad → \quad CaCl_2 \ + \ H_2O \ + \ CO_2$

Bubbles of carbon dioxide rise from marble chips dropped into acid. The stronger the acid, the faster the reaction happens.

EXPERIMENT: REACTIONS OF ACIDS AND CARBONATES

Problem

What gas is produced when acids react with carbonates?

Hypothesis

All carbonates contain carbon and oxygen, so the gas released may be carbon dioxide. This can be tested by seeing if the gas puts out a burning candle.

EQUIPMENT
- baking soda
- white vinegar
- bowl
- small candle
- modeling clay
- spoon

Experiment steps

1 Ask an adult to help you with this experiment. Stick a small candle upright on some modeling clay in the bottom of the bowl. Make sure that the wick is well below the level of the bowl's rim.

2 Carefully pour vinegar into the bowl so that the candle is surrounded, but not covered. Ask the adult to light the candle with a match.

3 Add half a teaspoon of baking soda to the vinegar and watch the flame carefully.

Results

What happens to the flame? What do you think caused this? Think about what would be produced in such a reaction. You can check your results on page 47.

Neutralizing acids and alkalis

A neutral liquid is a liquid that is neither an acid nor an alkali. It has a pH of 7. An acid or an alkali can be turned into a neutral liquid by a process called neutralization, which is a type of chemical reaction.

Neutralization happens when either an acid and a base, or an acid and an alkali, cancel each other out to make a neutral solution. The two most common neutralization reactions are between acids and bases called metal oxides, and between acids and alkalis called hydroxides. The products are always a salt and water. The general equation for these reactions is:

$$acid + base \rightarrow salt + water$$

Here is an example of the reaction between an acid and a hydroxide:

hydrochloric acid	+	sodium hydroxide	$\rightarrow$	sodium chloride	+	water
HCl	+	NaOH	$\rightarrow$	NaCl	+	H_2O

Here is an example of the reaction between an acid and a metal oxide:

hydrochloric acid	+	copper oxide	$\rightarrow$	copper chloride	+	water
2HCl	+	CuO	$\rightarrow$	$CuCl_2$	+	H_2O

Gradual neutralization

A base or an alkali only neutralizes an acid completely if enough of the base or alkali is added to the acid. If the base or alkali is added a little at a time, the solution gradually becomes less acidic, and eventually all the acid is neutralized and the solution is neutral. If more of the base is then added, the solution becomes alkaline.

EXPERIMENT: A NEUTRALIZATION REACTION

Problem

How can we neutralize an acid, making sure that it ends up completely neutral?

Hypothesis

By adding alkali gradually to the acid, and checking the pH of the solution, we can tell when the solution becomes neutral.

EQUIPMENT
- two jars or glasses
- measuring spoons
- measuring cup
- white vinegar
- baking soda
- red cabbage indicator (see page 15)

Experiment steps

1 Measure about 3 oz (100 ml) of water in the measuring cup, and pour the water into a glass. Dissolve one level teaspoon of baking soda in this water. This is your alkali.

2 Put two teaspoons of vinegar into the measuring cup, and add enough red cabbage indicator to get a nice red color. Top off the mixture with water to a total volume of 3 oz (100ml). Pour the colored mixture into the second glass. This is your acid.

3 Add one teaspoon of the colorless baking soda solution to your colored diluted vinegar, and stir. You may see some bubbles given off, but check the color of the mixture. Keep adding one teaspoon of bicarbonate of soda solution, stirring each time, until the mixture changes to a blue color. When this happens, the vinegar has been neutralized and some extra alkali has been added. Note how many teaspoons of the baking soda solution it took.

4 You now need to experiment to see exactly how much baking soda you need to get the mixture neutral. Wash out your colored mixture and make some fresh vinegar and indicator mixture following step 2. Repeat step 3, but stop before you add the last teaspoon. Add three-quarters of a teaspoon instead, and see if you get a blue color. If it turns blue, try the experiment again but add just a quarter of a teaspoon; if it does not turn blue, add another quarter of a teaspoon and see what happens. The goal is to get your experiment to the stage where just a little bit more baking soda solution would turn the mixture blue. You have neutralized the acid in the vinegar.

Results

Acids can be completely neutralized by alkalis using a suitable indicator.

Making salts

In chemistry, a salt is a substance made when an acid reacts with a base or an alkali. A salt is always a compound that contains a metal and a **nonmetal**. Common salt that we use in cooking is an example of a salt. Its chemical name is sodium chloride (NaCl), and it contains the metal sodium and the nonmetal chlorine. Other examples of salts are copper nitrate and iron sulfate.

A salt is made when the hydrogen in an acid is replaced by a metal. For example, when sodium replaces the hydrogen in hydrochloric acid, the salt sodium chloride is formed. When copper replaces the hydrogen in sulfuric acid, the salt copper sulfate is formed. Salts are named after the acid they are formed from. For example, sulfates are formed from sulfuric acid, chlorides from hydrochloric acid and nitrates from nitric acid.

Salts can be made by these four different reactions:

acid + metal	→	**salt + hydrogen**
acid + metal oxide (a base)	→	**salt + water**
acid + metal hydroxide (an alkali)	→	**salt + water**
acid + metal carbonate	→	**salt + water + carbon dioxide**

This salt-producing plant is the largest in Italy. It provides the country with 75 percent of all its salt.

EXPERIMENT: MAKING A SALT (SODIUM ETHANOATE)

Problem

How can we produce a salt?

Hypothesis

Salts are made when an acid reacts with an alkali or a base. We could try reacting a household acid and a household base together.

EQUIPMENT
- glass jar
- strainer and paper towel
- white vinegar
- baking soda
- teaspoon
- bowl
- saucepan

Experiment steps

1 Pour vinegar into a glass jar until it is about ½–1 inch (1–2 centimeters) deep.

2 Put half a teaspoon of baking soda into the vinegar and swirl or stir it to mix. When the fizzing stops, add another half teaspoon of baking soda, and mix again. If it still fizzes, add more baking soda until there is no more fizzing. You should have some baking soda left in the bottom of the jar at this stage.

3 Filter your mixture into a bowl, using the strainer lined with two layers of paper towel. The liquid that comes through (called the filtrate) should be clear. If you see any solid in it, filter again.

4 Leave the bowl on a window sill for a few days to let the water **evaporate**. Crystals of sodium ethanoate should appear. This is the best method to use because you will get bigger crystals. If you do not have several days to carry out step 4, and do not mind getting very small crystals, ask an adult to help you as described in step 5.

5 Ask an adult to boil a small pan of water with your bowl of filtrate on top. The adult should then adjust the heat to let the water in the pan simmer. When nearly all your filtrate has evaporated, let everything cool down.

Results

What has happened in the bowl? What do you think this substance is? You can check your results on page 47.

ACIDS IN THE ATMOSPHERE

The air in Earth's **atmosphere** is a mixture of gases. Roughly 99 percent of the air is made up of nitrogen and oxygen. In the remaining 1 percent is a very small amount of carbon dioxide. Carbon dioxide is an acidic gas that dissolves in water to make a weak acid called carbonic acid, which has a pH of about six. The carbon dioxide in the atmosphere dissolves in the water droplets that make up clouds and rain. This means that rainwater is always slightly acidic. As it flows over some metals and also some types of rock, it dissolves them. It also makes the ground it falls on slightly acidic.

Chemical weathering

Chemical weathering is the wearing away of the rocks of Earth's crust by this slightly acidic rain. Rocks such as limestone and chalk are made up mainly of calcium carbonate. When acidic rainwater flows over these rocks, it reacts with the calcium carbonate to form a salt called calcium hydrogencarbonate.

calcium carbonate	+	carbonic acid	→	calcium hydrogencarbonate
$CaCO_3$	+	H_2CO_3	→	$Ca(HCO_3)_2$

These stalagmites and stalactites have been formed as calcium carbonate has been deposited from calcium hydrogencarbonate.

The calcium hydrogencarbonate dissolves in water and is carried away, often creating huge underground caverns in limestone rocks. However, where water containing dissolved calcium hydrogencarbonate drips slowly from a surface, the reaction (shown in the box on page 30) can reverse, which means that calcium carbonate is deposited. Over many years, this can build up to form amazing rock formations called **stalagmites** and **stalactites**. The scale in a pot or pan is formed in the same way.

Acid rain

Scientists use the term acid rain to describe rainwater that is more acidic than natural rainwater. It is caused by **acidic gases** released into the atmosphere when **fossil fuels** are burned in factories, power stations, and vehicle engines. These gases include sulfur dioxide and oxides of nitrogen. When the gases dissolve in rainwater, they form acids that are stronger than carbonic acid.

Acid rain from burning fossil fuels is more harmful than natural rain because it dissolves rocks quickly and damages the stone on buildings and statues. It also reacts with metals such as steel, and weakens objects made from them. Acid rain can kill plants and animals, especially in areas where it falls regularly and flows into rivers and lakes. The amount of acidic gases released into the atmosphere can be reduced by devices such as catalytic converters in cars, or by removing impurities such as sulfur from fuels before they are used.

◀ The water in the soil around these plants has become strongly acidic because of acid rain. The trees cannot grow in these conditions.

USING ACIDS, BASES, AND ALKALIS

Many acids, alkalis, and bases are very useful. So are the reactions they take part in and the products of these reactions. We use these substances at home for cooking and cleaning, and in industry for processing materials and for making other chemicals.

Acid and alkali cleaners

Some cleaning liquids contain acids. **Descalers** are chemicals specifically designed to remove scale from inside pots and pans. Scale, sometimes called limescale, is a layer of calcium carbonate that has been deposited from tap water. It does not dissolve in water, so you cannot clean it away with water. It comes from the rocks that the water has flowed through. Acid in the descaler reacts with the scale, turning it into a salt called calcium hydrogencarbonate. This does dissolve in water, and gets washed away. Calcium hydrogencarbonate is a weak acid that does not react with the pot or water heater itself. Other household cleaners use stronger acids. They can be used to remove thick scale from materials that do not react with acids, such as glass and ceramics.

Strong alkalis such as sodium hydroxide are used in oven cleaners because they are very corrosive. They react with grease in the oven and turn it into simpler chemicals that can be washed away with water. Many soaps and detergents contain alkalis, too.

◀ This cleaner reacts with the dull silver oxide coating on silver, making it clean and shiny again.

The holes in bread are full of carbon dioxide gas created by reactions of acids and bases.

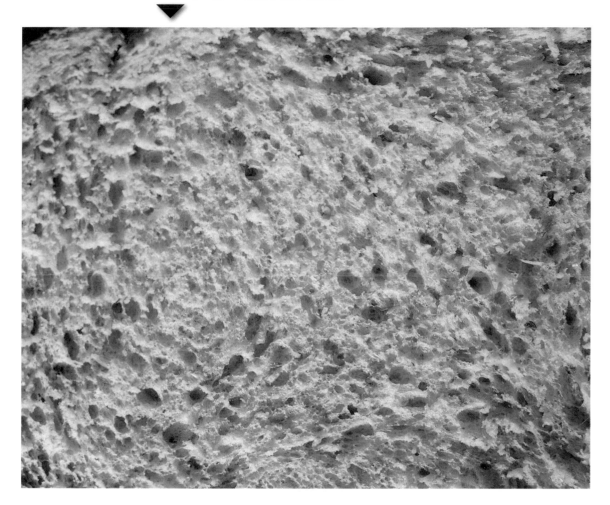

Acids and bases in cooking

Vinegar contains a weak acid called ethanoic acid. The **microorganisms** that feed on food and make it spoil cannot live in acid, so foods such as onions can be put in vinegar to preserve them. The vinegar soaks into the food, killing any microorganisms. This process of preserving food was very popular before refrigerators were invented.

Baking soda is an ingredient added to bread and cakes to make them rise. It contains the salt sodium hydrogencarbonate, also called sodium bicarbonate or bicarbonate of soda. When it is heated, it gives off carbon dioxide. This expands, making bubbles in the dough or cake mixture. Some baking powders also contain acidic solids. When the baking soda is mixed into a cake, it becomes wet. An acid is formed that reacts with the bicarbonate, and carbon dioxide is made.

Acids, bases, and alkalis in industry

Large amounts of acids, bases, and alkalis are made and used every year by industries. Acids, bases, and alkalis, and chemicals produced from them, are made at chemical plants. The plants are a maze of tanks and pipes, but they often do the same job as more simple equipment that you see in a laboratory—just on a much larger scale. Chemical reactions happen in the tanks, often at high temperatures and pressures, which makes the reactions happen faster and more efficiently.

Industrial acids

The most important industrial acid is sulfuric acid. It has many uses, such as cleaning and purifying metals, and making other industrial acids, such as phosphoric acids and nitric acid. Steel is cleaned thoroughly with sulfuric acid before it is galvanized (coated with zinc) to protect it from rusting.

The other main industrial acids are nitric acid and hydrochloric acid. Nitric acid is used to manufacture nitrate fertilizers and explosives such as nitroglycerin. Hydrochloric acid is used mainly for purifying metals.

This chemical plant in England produces chemicals, including sulfuric acid, which is used in detergents, soap, toothpaste, cement, and foams.

Industrial bases and alkalis

The most important industrial bases and alkalis are sodium hydroxide and sodium carbonate, both made from common salt (sodium chloride). Sodium hydroxide has many uses, such as making other chemicals, synthetic fibers, and soaps. The main use of sodium carbonate is in glassmaking.

Making fertilizers

Nitric acids and phosphoric acids are used to make fertilizers that farmers put on their fields to help crops grow better. The acids react with alkalis, such as ammonia, to make salts.

Fertilizer comes in pellets, like these. Farmers sprinkle the pellets on their fields, where they dissolve in rainwater and absorb into the soil.

MAKING SULFURIC ACID

Sulfuric acid is the most widely used chemical in industry. Hundreds of millions of tons of it are manufactured every year. Sulfuric acid is made using a process called the contact process. First, sulfur and oxygen are reacted together to make sulfur dioxide. This is then reacted with more oxygen, using a catalyst, to make sulfur trioxide. The sulfur trioxide is dissolved in sulfuric acid to make an extremely concentrated form of sulfuric acid called oleum. The oleum is stored, ready to be diluted to make acid for industry and laboratories.

Useful neutralization

As we have seen, neutralization is a chemical reaction in which an acid is neutralized by a base or an alkali, or in which an alkali is neutralized by an acid. Many acids, bases, and alkalis are used for neutralization reactions, which can be useful in everyday life.

Controlling acidity

One of the important properties of a soil is how acidic or alkaline it is. Different species of plants grow well in acidic soils, neutral soils, or alkaline soils. Gardeners and farmers often have to treat their soil to change its pH so that their crops will grow well.

Some soils have a pH as low as four or even three! To make soil less acidic, gardeners and farmers mix in a base called calcium oxide, which is also called lime or slaked lime. Lime is also added to land and lakes that have been made so acidic by acid rain that animals and plants are dying.

A farmer is spreading lime (calcium oxide) onto fields. Rain will wash the lime into the soil, reducing its acidity.

Treating stings

Insect and nettle plant stings hurt because the sting injects either acid or alkali into your skin. But they can be made less painful by neutralizing the acid or alkali. Bee, ant, and nettle plant stings are acidic, so you can treat them with an alkali. Wasp stings, on the other hand, contain alkali, so you can treat them with a weak acid such as vinegar. Never use strong laboratory acids on a sting!

EXPERIMENT: TESTING INDIGESTION TABLETS

Problem

Which antacid tablets neutralize hydrochloric acid best?

Hypothesis

Antacid tablets contain bases that neutralize excess hydrochloric acid in your stomach. Testing how much an indigestion tablet neutralizes a measured amount of acid will show how effective it is.

EQUIPMENT
- small jar
- white vinegar
- antacid tablets
- cabbage indicator (see page 15)
- piece of paper
- teaspoon

Experiment steps

1 Put one of the antacid tablets onto the paper. Fold the paper over the tablet and crush the tablet using the back of the teaspoon.
2 Pour some white vinegar into a small jar until the vinegar is roughly 1 inch (3 centimeters) deep. Add some cabbage indicator and make a note of the color of the mixture.
3 Open the paper, and use the tip of the teaspoon to add a small amount of crushed tablet to the jar. Watch the reaction and make a note of the color of the mixture.
4 Repeat steps 2 and 3 for each different brand of antacid tablet you have, using the same amount of vinegar each time.

5 You can extend your investigation by trying different tablets to see which ones neutralize the acids with the smallest amount of tablet (do this by adding small amounts of tablet until there is no further reaction). You can also try universal indicator solution or paper.

Results

Which tablet produces the greatest change in color? What do you think this means about its ability to neutralize acid? Check your results on page 47.

Useful salts

A salt is a compound containing a metal and a nonmetal, such as sodium chloride (common salt) and copper sulfate. All salts are made up of crystals, and they have a wide range of uses both at home and in industry. Here are a few examples.

Common salt

The salt that we put on food is common salt, and its chemical name is sodium chloride. As well as improving the flavor of some foods, it is an important part of our diet. It is also used for preserving food because, when it is very concentrated, it kills microorganisms. In industry, sodium chloride is used to make sodium hydroxide, sodium carbonate, chlorine, and hydrochloric acid. Rock salt is mostly sodium chloride, and it is spread on roads to keep them free of ice in cold weather.

FINDING SALT

Sodium chloride is obtained in two different ways—from seawater and by mining. Seawater is 2.7 percent sodium chloride, which is dissolved in the water. To get the sodium chloride from the water, the water is evaporated, leaving the salt behind. Most salt comes from mines. It is found in deposits called rock salt, and is dug out and crushed into powder by machines. Rock salt is also removed from the ground by pumping water into the rock. The salt dissolves in the water, which is pumped to the surface again and evaporated, leaving the salt behind.

These pools are called salt pans. Sea water is poured onto them, and salt is gradually left as the water evaporates.

Salts in medicine

If you have ever broken an arm or a leg, a salt called calcium sulfate may have been used to make your cast. Calcium sulfate is also known as plaster of Paris. Zinc carbonate, also known as calamine, is used to help soothe sore skin. Iron tablets contain iron sulfate, and the iron in them improves the way your blood carries oxygen around your body. Magnesium sulfate is an ingredient in constipation remedies.

Salts on the farm

All fertilizers are made up of salts, normally nitrates and phosphates made from nitric and phosphoric acids. The most common are ammonium nitrate, ammonium phosphate, sodium nitrate, and potassium nitrate. The salts contain nitrogen, phosphorus, and potassium, which the crops need to grow. Fertilizers come as pellets that are sprinkled on fields. They dissolve in rainwater and are washed into the soil, where they are absorbed by the plants' roots.

Phosphates and nitrates are used to manufacture explosives, such as the ones used in quarries.

THE PERIODIC TABLE

The periodic table is a chart of all the known elements. The elements are arranged in order of their atomic numbers, but in rows, so that elements with similar properties are underneath each other. The periodic table gets its name from the fact that the elements' properties repeat themselves every few elements, or periodically. The position of an element in the periodic table gives an idea of what its properties are likely to be.

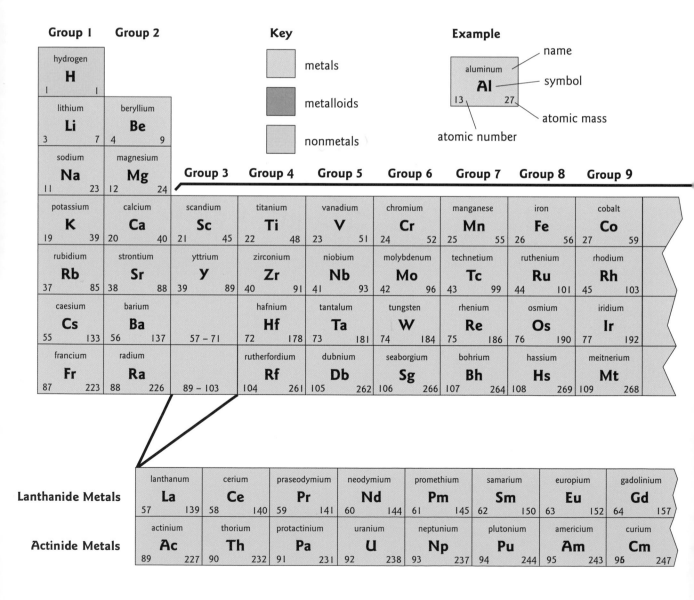

Groups and periods

The vertical columns of elements are called groups. The horizontal rows of elements are called periods. Some groups have special names:

Group 1: Alkali metals
Group 2: Alkaline earth metals
Groups 3–12: Transition metals
Group 17: Halogens
Group 18: Noble gases

The table is divided into two main sections, the metals and nonmetals. Between the two are elements that have some properties of metals and some of nonmetals. They are called semimetals or metalloids.

			Group 13	Group 14	Group 15	Group 16	Group 17	Group 18
								helium **He** 2 4
			boron **B** 5 11	carbon **C** 6 12	nitrogen **N** 7 14	oxygen **O** 8 16	fluorine **F** 9 19	neon **Ne** 10 20
Group 10	Group 11	Group 12	aluminum **Al** 13 27	silicon **Si** 14 28	phosphorus **P** 15 31	sulfur **S** 16 32	chlorine **Cl** 17 35	argon **Ar** 18 40
nickel **Ni** 28 59	copper **Cu** 29 64	zinc **Zn** 30 65	gallium **Ga** 31 70	germanium **Ge** 32 73	arsenic **As** 33 75	selenium **Se** 34 79	bromine **Br** 35 80	krypton **Kr** 36 84
palladium **Pd** 46 106	silver **Ag** 47 108	cadmium **Cd** 48 112	indium **In** 49 115	tin **Sn** 50 119	antimony **Sb** 51 122	tellurium **Te** 52 128	iodine **I** 53 127	xenon **Xe** 54 131
platinum **Pt** 78 195	gold **Au** 79 197	mercury **Hg** 80 201	thallium **Tl** 81 204	lead **Pb** 82 207	bismuth **Bi** 83 209	polonium **Po** 84 209	astatine **At** 85 210	radon **Rn** 86 222
darmstadtium **Ds** 110 281	roentgenium **Rg** 111 272	ununbium **Uub** 112 285	ununtrium **Uut** 113 284	ununquadium **Uuq** 114 289	ununpentium **Uup** 115 288	ununhexium **Uuh** 116 292		

terbium **Tb** 65 159	dysprosium **Dy** 66 163	holmium **Ho** 67 165	erbium **Er** 68 167	thulium **Tm** 69 169	ytterbium **Yb** 70 173	lutetium **Lu** 71 175
berkelium **Bk** 97 247	californium **Cf** 98 251	einsteinium **Es** 99 252	fermium **Fm** 100 257	mendelevium **Md** 101 258	nobelium **No** 102 259	lawrencium **Lr** 103 262

Common elements

Here is a table of the most common elements from the periodic table that you may come across at home or in the laboratory. The table indicates whether the element is a metal, nonmetal, or metalloid, and whether it is a solid, liquid, or gas at room temperature.

Element	Symbol	Metal or not	State at room temperature
hydrogen	H	nonmetal	gas
helium	He	nonmetal	gas
lithium	Li	metal	solid
carbon	C	nonmetal	solid
nitrogen	N	nonmetal	gas
oxygen	O	nonmetal	gas
fluorine	F	nonmetal	gas
neon	Ne	nonmetal	gas
sodium	Na	metal	solid
magnesium	Mg	metal	solid
aluminum	Al	metal	solid
silicon	Si	metalloid	solid
phosphorus	P	nonmetal	solid
sulfur	S	nonmetal	solid
chlorine	Cl	nonmetal	gas
argon	Ar	nonmetal	gas
potassium	K	metal	solid
calcium	Ca	metal	solid
iron	Fe	metal	solid
copper	Cu	metal	solid
zinc	Zn	metal	solid
bromine	Br	nonmetal	liquid
silver	Ag	metal	solid
tin	Sn	metal	solid
iodine	I	nonmetal	solid
gold	Au	metal	solid
mercury	Hg	metal	liquid
lead	Pb	metal	solid

Common chemicals

Here is a table of some common chemicals that you may find at home or in your school's science class. The column on the right shows their chemical formulas.

Gases	
hydrogen	H_2
oxygen	O_2
chlorine	Cl_2
nitrogen	N_2
carbon dioxide	CO_2
nitrogen dioxide	NO_2
Liquids and solutions	
water	H_2O
hydrochloric acid	HCl
sulfuric acid	H_2SO_4
nitric acid	HNO_3
sodium hydroxide	$NaOH$
Solids	
sodium chloride	$NaCl$
magnesium oxide	MgO
calcium carbonate	$CaCO_3$
copper sulfate	$CuSO_4$

Common acids, bases, and alkalis

This list gives the uses of the most common acids, bases, and alkalis.

hydrochloric acid HCl	Regulation of the pH of liquids, neutralization of alkalis, surface cleaning of iron and steel before processing, production of salts, such as calcium chloride and zinc chloride, production of compounds, such as PVC and other plastics, active ingredient in household cleaners, manufacture of food additives such as citric acid and gelatin. Found naturally in stomach.
sulfuric acid H_2SO_4	Manufacture of phosphoric acid, surface cleaning of iron and steel before processing, general use in chemical industry, use in accumulator batteries (e.g., car batteries), active ingredient in drain cleaners. Found naturally in acid rain.
nitric acid HNO_3	Used in manufacture of fertilizers and explosives, used in manufacture of aqua regia (liquid that can dissolve gold and platinum). Found naturally in acid rain.
phosphoric acid H_3PO_4	Used in removal of rust from iron and steel, used in laboratories to test for substances and for producing other substances, additive in food and drink, used for etching.
acetic acid/ ethanoic acid $C_2H_4O_2$	Used in production of some plastics, glues, and paints, used in manufacture of solvents for inks and paints, a food additive (used in vinegar), used in laboratories to test for substances and for producing other substances.
citric acid $C_6H_8O_7$	A food additive (flavoring and preservative), as a replacement for lemon juice in cooking, used in manufacture of food supplements, used in cleaners, soaps, and detergents, used in water softeners. Found naturally in citrus fruits.
sodium hydroxide (caustic soda) NaOH	Used in neutralization of acids, manufacture of pulp and paper, soap manufacture, production of biodiesel fuel, etching of aluminum, food processing, as an active ingredient in drain cleaners.
calcium hydroxide (slaked lime) $Ca(OH)_2$	Used to improve acid soils, water and sewage treatment, an ingredient in building mortar and plaster, used to neutralize acids, as a dental cleaner, and in manufacture of pesticides.
potassium hydroxide (caustic potash) KOH	Used to improve acid soils, used as a fungicide and herbicide, used in paper making, as a catalyst, for the neutralization of acids, used in alkaline batteries.
ammonia NH_3	Used in manufacture of nitric acid, in production of fertilizers and explosives, in manufacture of plastics, active ingredient in household cleaners, used as a refrigerant. Found naturally in rainwater.

GLOSSARY OF TECHNICAL TERMS

acidic gas gas that dissolves in water to make an acid. Hydrogen chloride is an acidic gas. It dissolves in water to make hydrochloric acid.

alkaline liquid that has a pH above 7. All alkalis are alkaline. Alkaline also describes solids or gases that dissolve in water to make alkalis. For example, sodium is an alkaline metal. It dissolves in water to produce an alkali.

atmosphere thick blanket of air that surrounds Earth

atom extremely tiny particles of matter. An atom is the smallest particle of an element that can exist. All substances are made up of atoms.

carbonate compound made up of atoms of one element combined with another group of atoms made up of one carbon atom and three oxygen atoms

caustic substance that corrodes or burns

chemical formulas collection of symbols and numbers that represents an element or compound. It shows what elements are in a compound and the ratio of the numbers of atoms of each element.

chemical reaction when two chemicals (called the reactants) react together to form new chemicals (called the products)

compound substance made up of two or more elements that are joined together by chemical bonds

concentrated acid solution that contains a large amount of acid dissolved in it

corrosive chemical that eats away other substances. Strong acids and strong alkalis are corrosive.

descaler chemical that removes scale that has formed inside water containers such as pots and pans

detergent chemical that breaks down oil and grease. Detergents are used for cleaning, and are contained in dishwashing liquids and laundry soaps.

digestion process of breaking down food into simple substances that the body can use

dilute acid solution that contains a small amount of solute compared to the amount of water in it

displacement reaction chemical reaction in which one of the elements in a compound is pushed out or displaced from the compound by another element. Some metals displace the hydrogen in an acid when they are put in the acid.

element substance that contains just one type of atom. Elements are the simplest substances that exist.

evaporate change from liquid to gas at a temperature below the liquid's boiling point

fertilizer chemical that contains elements such as nitrogen and potassium, that plants need to grow. Farmers spread fertilizers on their fields to make their crops grow better.

fossil fuel natural fuel such as coal or gas, formed over thousands of years from the remains of living things

indicator substance that changes color to show whether the liquid it is put in is acidic or alkaline. Some indicators also show how strongly acidic or alkaline a liquid is.

insoluble base base that does not dissolve in water. Insoluble bases can still neutralize acids.

litmus chemical extracted from lichens that acts as an indicator. Red litmus paper turns blue in an alkali. Blue litmus paper turns red in an acid.

metal any element in the periodic table that is shiny, and that conducts electricity and heat well. Most metals are also hard.

microorganism living thing too small to see without a microscope

neutralize chemical reaction in which an acid or an alkali becomes a neutral liquid. Acids are neutralized by alkalis and bases. Alkalis are neutralized by acids.

nonmetal any element in the periodic table that is not a metal. Most nonmetals are gases.

organism single living thing

pH scale of the acidity or alkalinity of a liquid. A liquid with a pH less than 7 is an acid. A liquid with a pH greater than 7 is an alkali. A liquid with a pH of 7 is neutral.

properties characteristics of a substance, such as its strength, melting point, and density

raw materials substances that are the starting point for manufacturing. For example, oil is the raw material used in the production of plastic bags.

reactivity series list of common metals, arranged in order of how quickly they react with other substances, such as acids, water, and air. The most reactive metals are at the top.

salt substance made when an acid reacts with an alkali or a base. A salt is always a compound that contains a metal and one or more nonmetals.

solution liquid made when a substance (the solute) dissolves in a liquid (the solvent)

stalactite columns of calcium carbonate that grow down from the roof of a cave

stalagmite columns of calcium carbonate that grow up from the floor of a cave

universal indicator indicator that shows the strength of an acid or alkali. Universal indicator comes in paper and liquid form.

FURTHER READING

e. science encyclopedia. New York: DK Publishing, 2004.

Gardner, Robert. *Chemistry Science Fair Projects: Using Acids, Bases, Metals, Salts, and Inorganic Stuff.* New York: Enslow, 2004.

Johnson, Rebecca. *Acids and Bases.* Washington D.C.: National Geographic, 2004.

Parsons, Jayne. *The Way Science Works.* New York: DK Publishing, 2002.

Useful websites

http://www.chem4kids.com
A lot of information and activities on chemistry, presented in a fun way.

http://www.chemicalelements.com
An interactive Periodic table. Originally created, in 1996, as an 8th grade science project.

http://www.creative-chemistry.org.uk
An interactive chemistry site including fun practical activities, worksheets, quizzes, puzzles, and more!

http://www.heinemannexplore.com
An online resource for school libraries and classrooms containing articles, investigations, biographies, and activities related to all areas of the science curriculum.

http://www.webelements.com/
webelements/scholar
The Periodic table – online! Discover more about all the elements and their properties.

Experiment results

page 15: The cabbage juice turns a different color in the tap water and in the weak acid. This shows that it works as an indicator.

page 20–21: When you hold the flame over the mouth of the tube you should hear a popping sound. This shows that the gas produced was hydrogen, which burned when the flame was close to it. Hydrogen often burns so quickly that it explodes—this is the popping sound you hear. When metals react with acids, they produce hydrogen.

page 23: The zinc nail will fizz most quickly, so it is the most reactive. Iron will fizz a little bit, and the copper nail will not fizz at all. It is the least reactive.

page 25: The flame should go out. This is caused by the gas produced during the reaction. The carbonate contains carbon and oxygen. Carbon dioxide does not support burning, so the gas is probably carbon dioxide.

page 29: Crystals of a solid will form in the bowl. This solid must be the salt sodium acetate formed in the reaction between the acetic acid in the vinegar and the sodium bicarbonate in the baking soda.

page 37: The tablet that produces the greatest change in color is the best at neutralizing the acid.

INDEX